T0193375

turmeric milk

aleema garfinkel

To order additional copies of this book, contact:
Xlibris
844-714-8691
www.Xlibris.com
Orders@Xlibris.com

ISBN: Softcover   978-1-6698-1768-0
             EBook   978-1-6698-1767-3

Print information available on the last page

Rev. date: 04/05/2022

to all the women who held me hope
and offered me the gold
to glue my broken parts back together
you showed me that all along
i was art
kintsugi

i don't feel safe in my own head
when it's not a sauna of brain fog,
it's a chaotic battlefield of blues
i am a bystander in an ongoing conflict
between my brain and body—
while my body is just doing its job to keep me
alive, healthy, and nourished,
my brain is trying to keep me
hurting, starving, and barely living
i have trust issues with my own mind

everything i believe
is murky with conflicting beliefs
each role, an additional weight
pulling me further into shambles
i am a venn diagram,
lost in between too many roles,
till i have no solid identity left

depression holds my hand
too tightly to feel another's touch
she loosens her grip in moments of joy,
yet her fingers brush a constant awareness
of the fleetingness of happiness

dirt fragments minutely momentously shift

roots elongate spreading their fingers

threading their presence into the ground

the smallest spark of green

emerges from the dark damp earth

no number of breeze nor bird

may invalidate belittle negate

the statement she has planted into the soil

an ode to growth

my body tremors in effort

no sound escapes my mouth

worry lines frame my face

cheeks wet my pillowcase with pain

knees bunch up like a fetus

in a blanket cocoon womb

my arms lace around my waist

holding onto myself for dear life

as i heave out a desperate

cry for help

scars that ridge my skin,
a sour taste in my mouth,
and a face aged beyond my years;
i crumple thinking of all the pain
i held and invalidated
as i spilt my blood, guts, and tears
like it was just something to do

every nerve in my body is lit on fire
aching itching screaming for relief
from the shackles of these hospital walls
the ever-watching eyes watching watching watching
watching me eat watching me sleep watching me pee
a million insects thrash under my skin
begging groaning pleading to be freed
runaway

i spend too much time analyzing
the way every bite i take
will translate to the way my body looks
food is not nourishment,
it's a number
a number of calories
a number on a scale
a number of worth i give myself

my body holds me taught

trapped in place

as my mind yanks open my lids

forcing my eyes witness to

pain pain pain

a hundred miles an hour my heart races

as the tape in my head plays

over and over and over

mold in the corner of the bathtub

a dying plant in my therapist's waiting room

the droning radio on the car ride back home

stubborn dirt under my fingernails

a frayed letter at the bottom of a drawer

not recognizing the face in my mirror

depression is

when i was little, i would picture my shaadhi:

the way my bridal lengha would flow,

how heavy my nath would feel on my nose,

and who my bridesmaids would be.

now, i wonder:

how much mendhi is necessary to cover limbs full of scars,

if i will ever be able to fall in love with a man,

and how much dowry is enough for a mentally ill bride.

my mind slowed and blurred;
not only food, but
memories, panic, pain,
i restrict.
my sight blackened if i move too quick;
not only food, but
the desperation to be seen,
i purge.
my frame edged by bone;
not only food, but
the space i take up,
i constrict.

lungs burning in rhythm with your feet pounding a bit too hard
　　　　there is no feeling
a bit too many pills sloshing in your vodka-filled stomach
　　　　　closer to
swimming out a bit too far into the vicious ocean current
　　　　　farther from
pressing a bit too firmly on the blade at your wrist
　　　　　　freedom

you say you like my boldness,
as you look past my quaking
to get to my body
i let you help yourself to me,
shattering the broken pieces
i had worked so hard to glue together
you didn't know better,
as any ceasing words
stayed a shape on my lips,
held back by my own low self-esteem,
my own loss of morals,
my own addiction to hurt

a dark cloak envelops me
in security, comfort, control
she covers my eyes
too blind at times
and squeezes me tight
too tight at times
still, how can you ask me
to shed my lover's hold
after her being
all i've ever known

is it alright if i crawl into your bed like i used to

is it alright if you braid my hair like you used to

is it alright if i wipe my nose on your chaadar like i used to

is it alright if you hold my hand like you used to

is it alright if i pick you flowers like i used to

is it alright if you call me beta like you used to

is it alright is it alright is this alright am i alright

time and change make me feel like i'm on a little boat
afloat a vast and unpredictable ocean
it's all i can do to stay afloat through all its waves,
much less move forward by my own will
i'm sinking

i stand stripped and shivering

as yet another nurse draws a copy of the scars on my body

i think of the way detectives examine cadavers

and my body crumples from shame and exhaustion—

i am exhausted from having stolen from me

a part of me that i hid from the world for so long

my heart thuds in symphony with yours
as my head rests against your chest
my ear a stethoscope to your pain
oh how i wish i could reach in between your ribs
scoop her up and plead for her to beat easy
beat easier, little heart, beat easier
instead, i wrap my arms around you
and squeeze just a bit tighter
hoping my love floods in from my embrace
and envelops her entirely with its intention

i scrub my hands and lick my wounds
wiping the residue that lingers on my skin
from your sticky fingers' touch
i wring myself raw, and still,
your fingerprints remain
embedded in my soul
i wilt from effort to undo
the stains you produced
generational trauma

hair sticks sweatily to my face

breathe i can't breathe

eyes spew pain, fingernails dig in palms

please don't be mad at me

panic courses through my veins

get off of me

as i kick and thrash the trauma out of them

no please stop

how can i consciously know i am present

am i crazy

and yet subconsciously be so far away?

i felt the warm sand shift to accept my body's shape–
but it may as well have felt like numbness
i tasted the salt carried in the breeze–
but it may as well have tasted like indifference
i listened to the waves crash and children squeal–
but it may as well have sounded like emptiness
i smelled sunscreen, spritzers, saltwater–
but it may as well have smelled like dread
i saw orange as my eyes squint heed to the sun–
but it may as well have been dark
depression stole my senses

the world is so big
but you made it feel so small.
for a while, the smallness sustained me,
containing and contorting all my parts
to minimize them—
to minimize me.
finally, the parts gasped
as i fled the constraints.
and yet, without the constraints,
without you,
i spilled and spewed,
scrambling to find new limits
to hold me as i outgrew your limits—
outgrew you.
i only wish you could see
the ways in which you limited me.
we've been breathing the same air for too long,
and only now are my lungs fully filled.

i wish i could disappear

so seamlessly

to leave no ripple

in the flow of the lives around me

like a fallen tree

that no one heard fall

a seedless fruit

bruised, fed on, forgotten

weighted down
and rooted to my mattress
my body has become
    too
        heavy
for me to carry
or maybe my mind has become
    too
        weak

please hold my head in your lap

don't critique the color i dyed my hair this time

cut me fruit don't shame the ways i've cut my skin

look at what you did to yourself

tell me stories as i sit on the kitchen counter watching you cook

listen to me are you listening to me were you ever listening to me

let me cry in your arms please don't tell me

there's nothing for you to be crying about

braid my long hair for me ow please don't pull so tight

run your fingers through my hair wait no stop

why are you crying why am i crying

your veined hands working prayer beads mesmerize my big eyes

please don't taunt me for the ways i'm doing religion wrong

cover yourself up besharmi

the smell of your desi curries fragrance our home

stop commenting on the ways my body has changed

you are seated by my hospital bed when i gain consciousness crying

how could you be so ungrateful to god how could you how could you

tell me you love me do you love me please don't say you love me

your words hold daggers to my demise drowning me drowning me

they hold so much weight to me why do they hold so much weight to me

am i such a bad mother that i didn't know

there was something wrong with my own daughter

and even still your silence stings sharper through the stale air

i can't stand being in the same room as you for one more breath

i have never loved and yearned for anyone as deeply as i do you

mama

in the same way the monstera grows beauty
in every hole she designs,
in the same way the moon still shines light
in all of her phases,
in the same way i still water my plants
when they wilt in the grim of winter,
i'm learning to be kind to myself
in all of my seasons

and with my finger shoved down my throat,
       i feel the *guilt* of
1 in 6 americans not knowing where their next meal will come from,
       as my previous one comes back up
the hours of work my dad has put in to pay for my meal plan,
       as i panic over trips to the dining hall
the emaciated child with a rumbling belly in a third world country,
       while mine pangs for the food my pantry is full of

i am a ten-year-old twenty-year-old

crying herself to sleep and wetting her sheets

craving her mama in a way she's never known her to be

i am a ten-year-old twenty-year-old

shaking scared swimming in a hospital gown five sizes too big

yearning for a hand to hold her own

i am a ten-year-old twenty-year-old

melting at the softness of any and every woman

yet resenting them for being unable to satisfy the pit in her stomach

too often i find myself
gasping for air
as if i got so caught up in
productivity
that i forgot to
breathe

mornings are for fresh starts

as every other college student showers off

their friday night hangovers, i shower off

the shame of relapses

that drip red down the drain,

that suffocate me with

their hot metallic-scented steam,

and stubbornly stain

my morning-afters

solid, existent, observant

my roots, though frayed, run deep

my bark, though blemished, holds steady

my branches, though weeping, nestle life

my tree rings, though narrow, print growth

dendrochronology

you crush vile pills in honey
and shove them down my throat
no longer will i swallow
your masqueraded bitterness
no longer will i swallow and smile
i spit back bile dripping resentment
and i bite the hands that feed me
individuating

i pour myself into checks off to-do lists
to give me a sense of moving forward,
neatly outlined schedules
to organize the mess my mind hands me,
and plans for every detail of the rest of my life,
when today feels like too much to stay present in
this is how i cope

my eyes leak the pain
of every existence i've ever laid them on
my body shakes the burden
of all the souls i could not save
my heart thumps the hurt
of weariness and worry
empath

i choke on words and tears years overdue

my lungs can't pump oxygen fast enough

to keep up with how fast my mind is going

pale blue walls spin around me in a blur

the warmth of the hospital blanket is suddenly unbearable

i feel detached from the person the band on my wrist says i am

i flush from the shame that accompanies a malfunctioning mind

and the only words i can manage to string together are a desperate

i'm fine!

1. your "crocodile tears" are beautiful, reasonable, accurate reactions to your world

2. you shouldn't have to fake stomach aches to feel cared for

3. there is nothing shameful about hairy legs or showing your skin

4. i'm sorry your cheeks were pinched raw (and your boundaries violated)

5. you shouldn't have had to learn to dissociate to bear the yelling

6. you are not "mota"

7. no amount of "A"s will be worth the insane pressure you put on yourself

8. you are not a sinner for liking her

9. the world is not designed for you

10. but that doesn't mean you are less worthy of taking up space in it

ten things i would tell my inner child

when i was little, my dad would play a game
in which he would squeeze my little suntanned hand
       one
             two
                  three
and i would squeeze his big calloused hand back
       one
            two
               three
now i lie clenching and unclenching my hands
trying to remember what being alive feels like
       one
the tornado in my mind whisks me back
            two
to the days of root beer floats, book fairs, and bugbites
               three
when carefully, strategically squeezing back three times
was the greatest task i had to overcome
to win my parents' pride

shame envelops my existence
in every pill i must swallow,
every therapy i must try,
every facility i must stay at.
i feel permanently branded,
hot iron searing it into my skin:
the type of person who ends up in a psych ward

six feet deep

blinded by fog i can't see

intertwined by root i can't move

fed on by bug i can't live

hold my hand hold me hope

will you hold my hand

hold my hand hold me hope

hold me hope so i know

i can lean in to stay afoot

one foot in the grave

and despite the acceptance i will never find in them,
the comfort combed through my head
by my mother's hands
my weary mind nestled beside her
her familiar english-urdu in my ears
her rose-scented lotion
and the rough feel of her cotton salwar kameez
no other place feels more like
home

my resume is lined with threads of
hardworking, driven, and well-rounded.
under which section do i add
overcommitted, exhausted, and burnt out?

place a magnifying glass to my mind where
poisonous mushrooms and carnivorous venuses
raid every ounce of my existence
suffocating vines and murky swamp water
intently muddy my insides
for every effort to prune or slash
dozens more stake their claim
my head is a jungle

do you have any idea how gut-wrenchingly dehumanizing it is

to be stripped and scanned, eyes consuming every inch of you

to have the hinges tire at your door being constantly and incessantly swung open

to have your belongings stolen, for fear of their becoming tools to your destruction

to have the sound of 911 receptors and sirens embedded in your head

to have your drawers searched and your pills counted

to be shaken awake to ensure you're alive

to have your every bite surveillanced

to have to count in the restroom

to be looked at with eyes that gleam with pity and desperation

to be labeled a danger and to be stripped of any trust

to be whispered about rather than talked to

to be stamped with a diagnosis not a name

to be a problem not a person

and worst of all,

to not be able to protest,

because this is nothing but the treatment you deserve?

stems replace my bones,

leaves are the hair that coats my skin,

my sweat the morning dew

each breath roots me further into the ground

how will i uphold strength

if i let my sap spill over everyone?

how can i expect to flower

if i don't nourish my herbaceous heart?

how will i stay rooted

if i push away those who water my soil?

how do i expect to heal

if i don't turn my sunflower soul to the sun?

i cupped my messiness
like water in my hands
held close to my body
i'm sorry i let you
get so close that
it spilled on you

from the back of the ambulance,

my eyes witnessed the sun rise.

as oranges and pinks flooded the sky,

my favorite time of day

made me feel nothing.

my senses received no response from my mind;

my inner world disconnected from the outer world.

somber, strapped down, streams dripped

from my nose my chin

morning person

vomit covered finger

a Walmart grocery bag in my lap

tears smudge mascara

gluing my lashes to each other

i can't see

blades yanked out of razors

collect in my drawers

red stains

tissues, towels, sheets

i don't see

pill bottles line my windowsill

go to pharmacy, check

medicate me, check

cure me,

i won't see

a look around my room

i am not suicidal in the way

pain violently shreds through every ounce of a soul

i am suicidal in the way

blood slows and skin numbs to a winter's cold

i'm bored of nourishing my flesh suit

i'm bored of brushing the bones that pulp my sustenance

i'm bored of washing the collection of cells that sprout from my head

i'm bored of participating in the pursuit of capital

i'm bored of shoving enough media into my mind to be deemed "cultured"

i'm bored of being a pathetic screw in the massive machinery of a world

the concept of existing simply bores me

leaving warm handprints on cold windows

"this made me think of you" texts

running barefoot in the grass

surprise hugs from behind

letting snow melt on your tongue

writing in book margins

taking the long way home

kissing it better

letting paint get on my hands

singing in the shower

i believe in

coconut oil in my hair
to catch the clumps it falls in
a nazar necklace around my neck
to ward off the evil eye's grasp
and haldhi doodh on my tongue
to heal my deeply wounded soul
south asian ssri

and if not for all the beautiful women

who carried me when i refused to carry myself

who wove their love into baskets to hold my broken pieces

who wore masks of strength when mine fell off

and who delicately sat with me through all my lows–

if not for them, if not for you,

i would have never lived to see another high

thank you

here i am

after spending all of twenty years

attempting to attain perfection

to attain "normal"

to attain worth

here i am

here i am fighting my hands from slitting my skin

here i am fighting my mouth to swallow food

here i am fighting my mind to be present

here i (barely) am

Printed in the United States
by Baker & Taylor Publisher Services